Fantasy World

Vol. 2

GRAYSCALE PHOTO COLORING BOOK FOR ADULTS

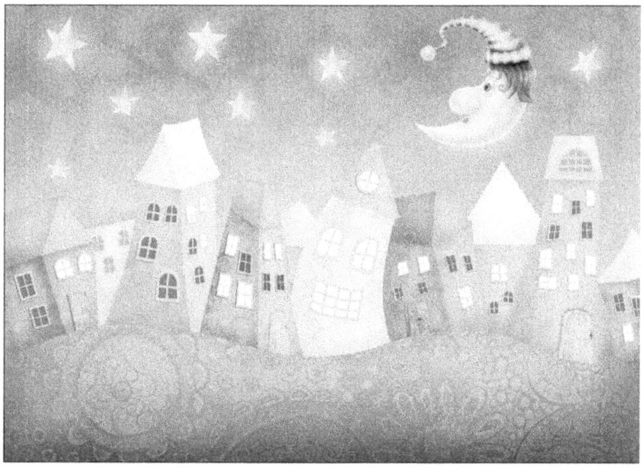

Majestic COLORING

www.MajesticColoring.com

ISBN: 978-1533591388

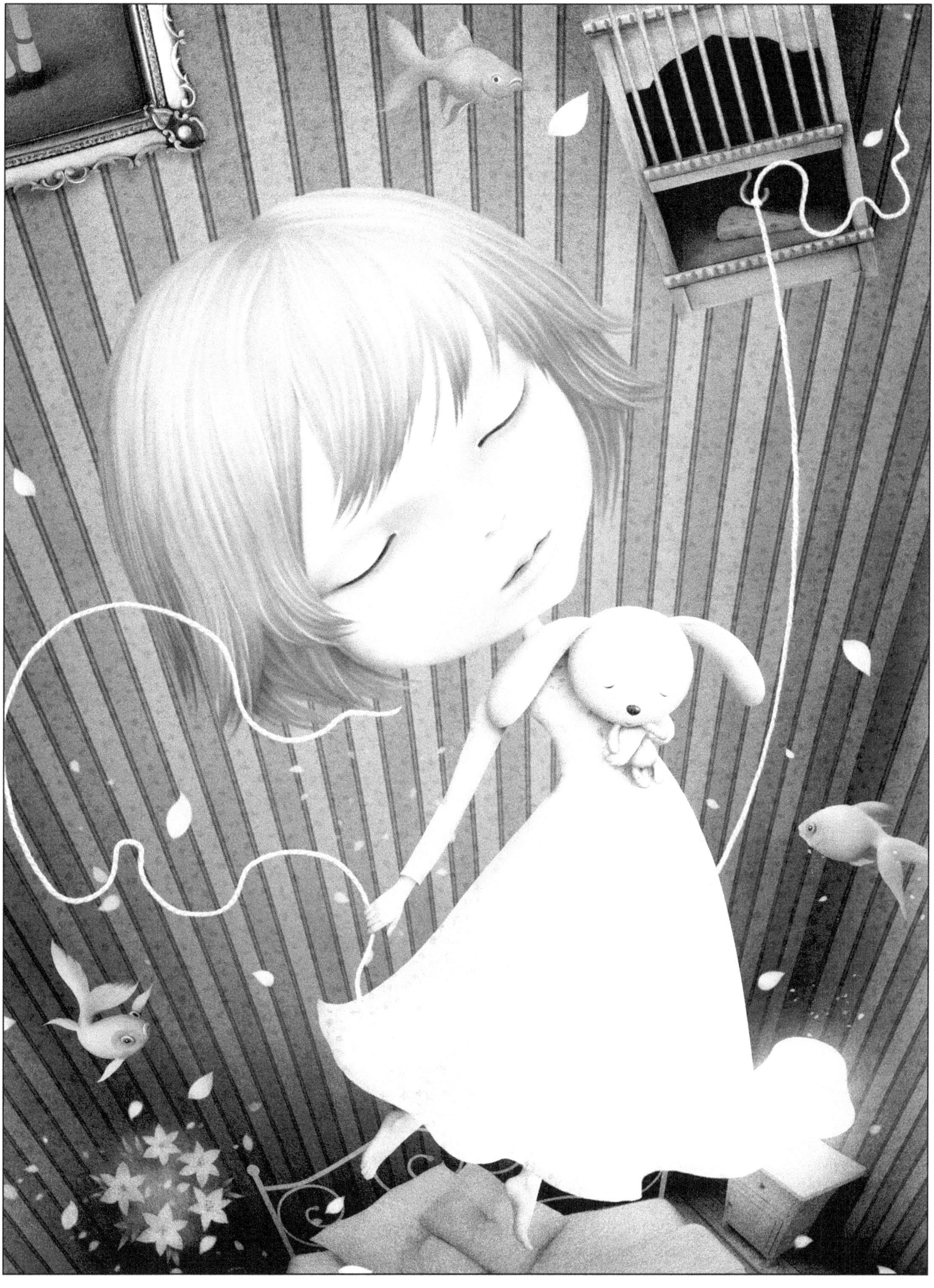

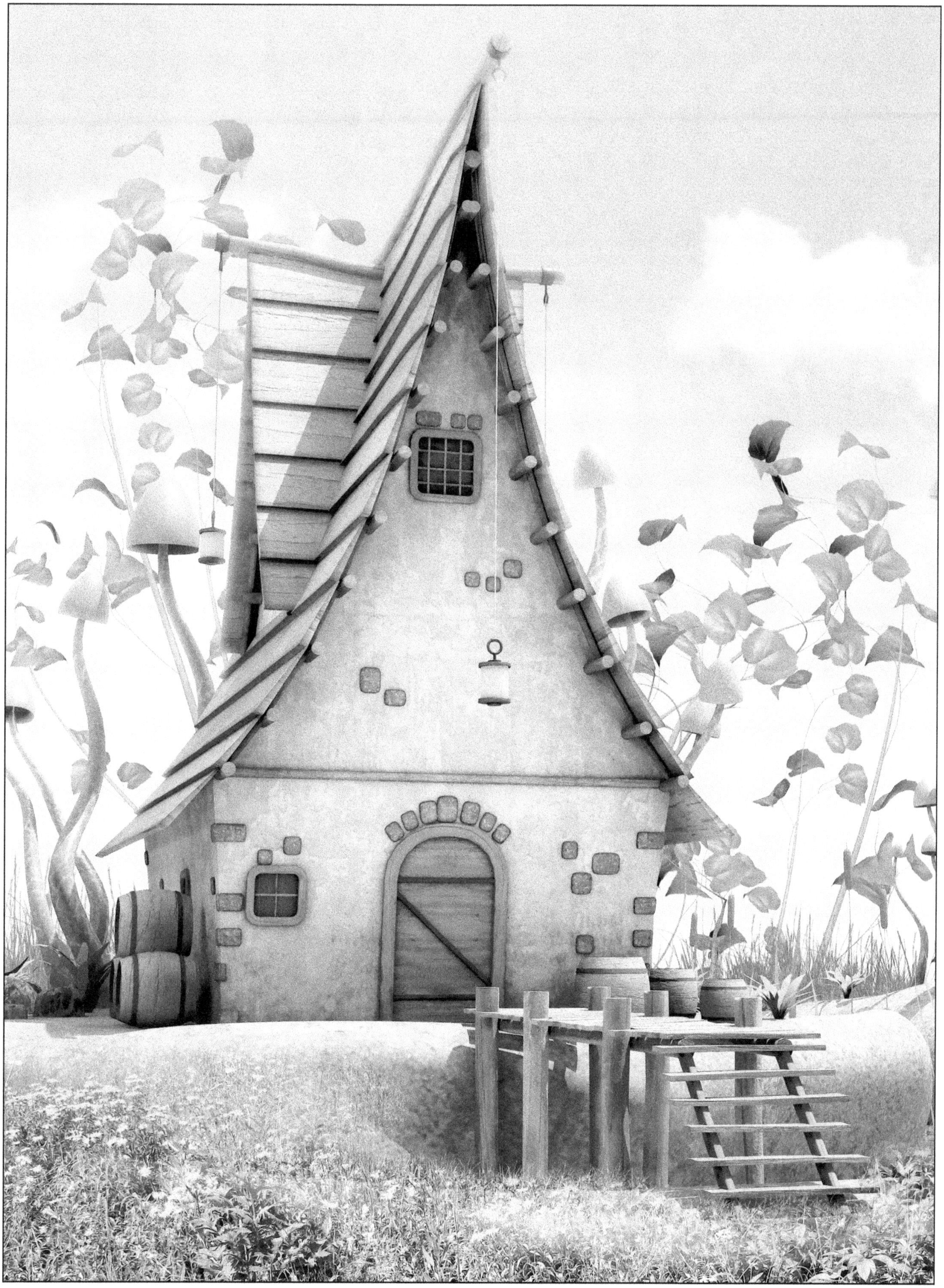

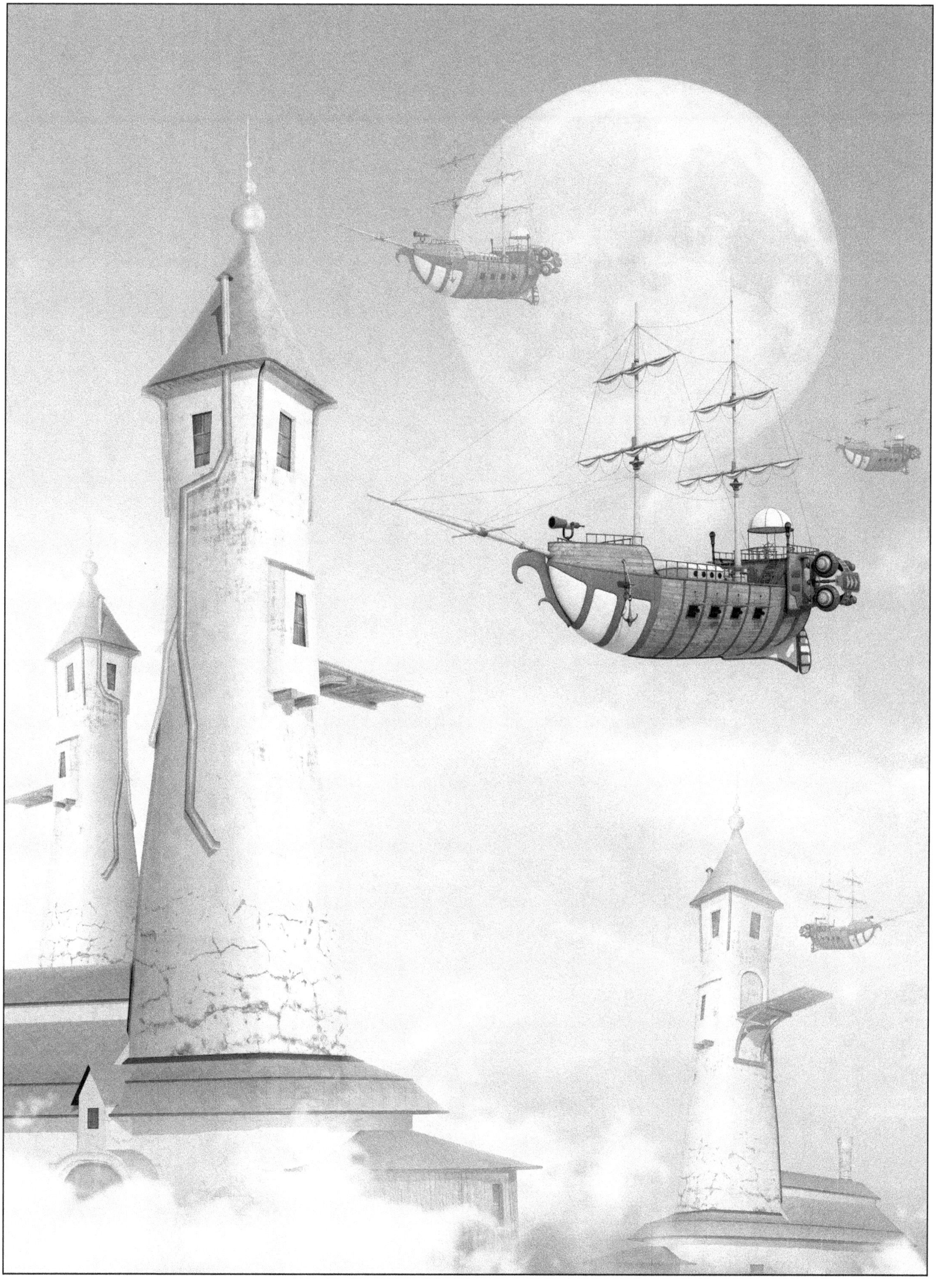

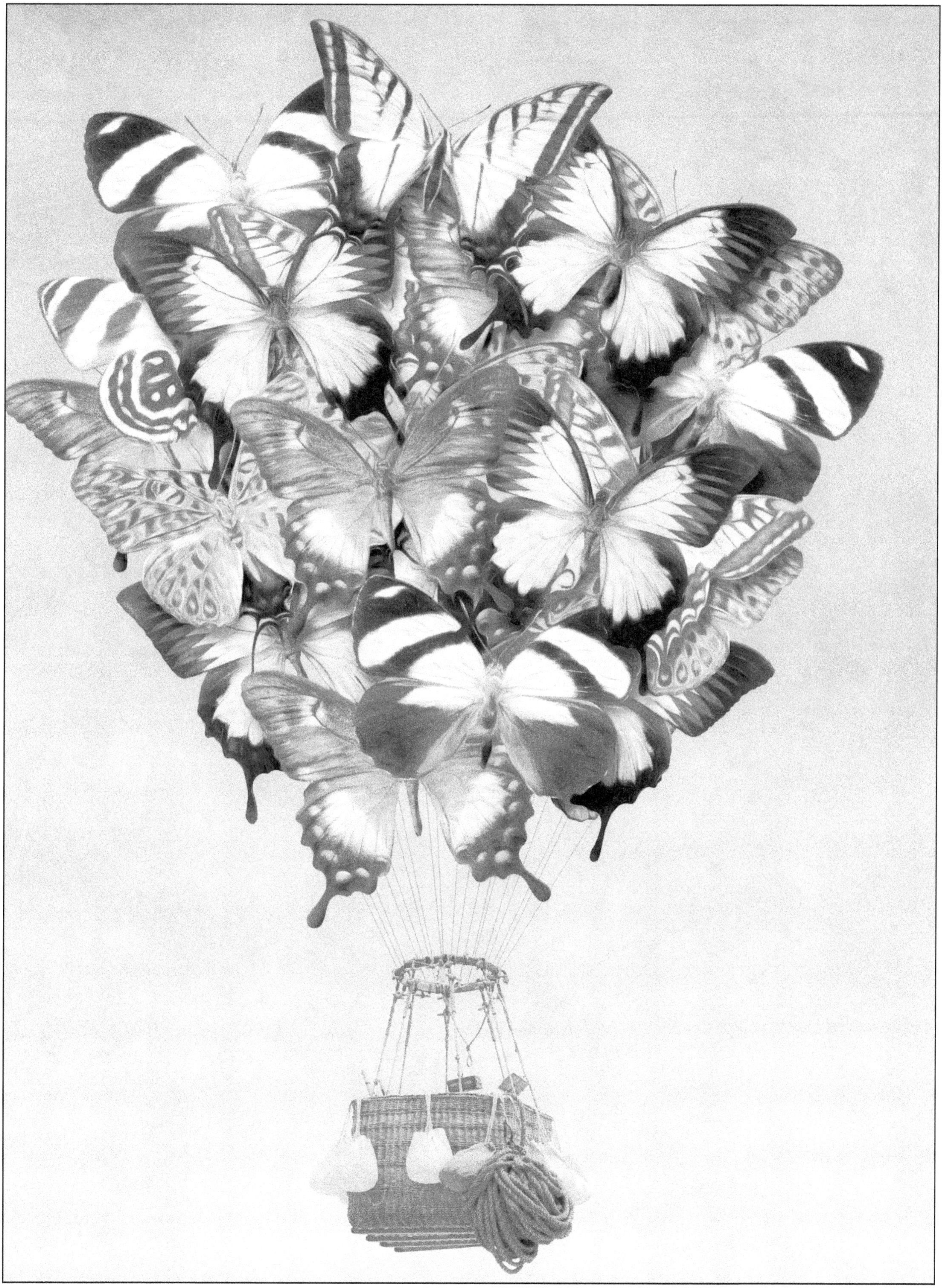

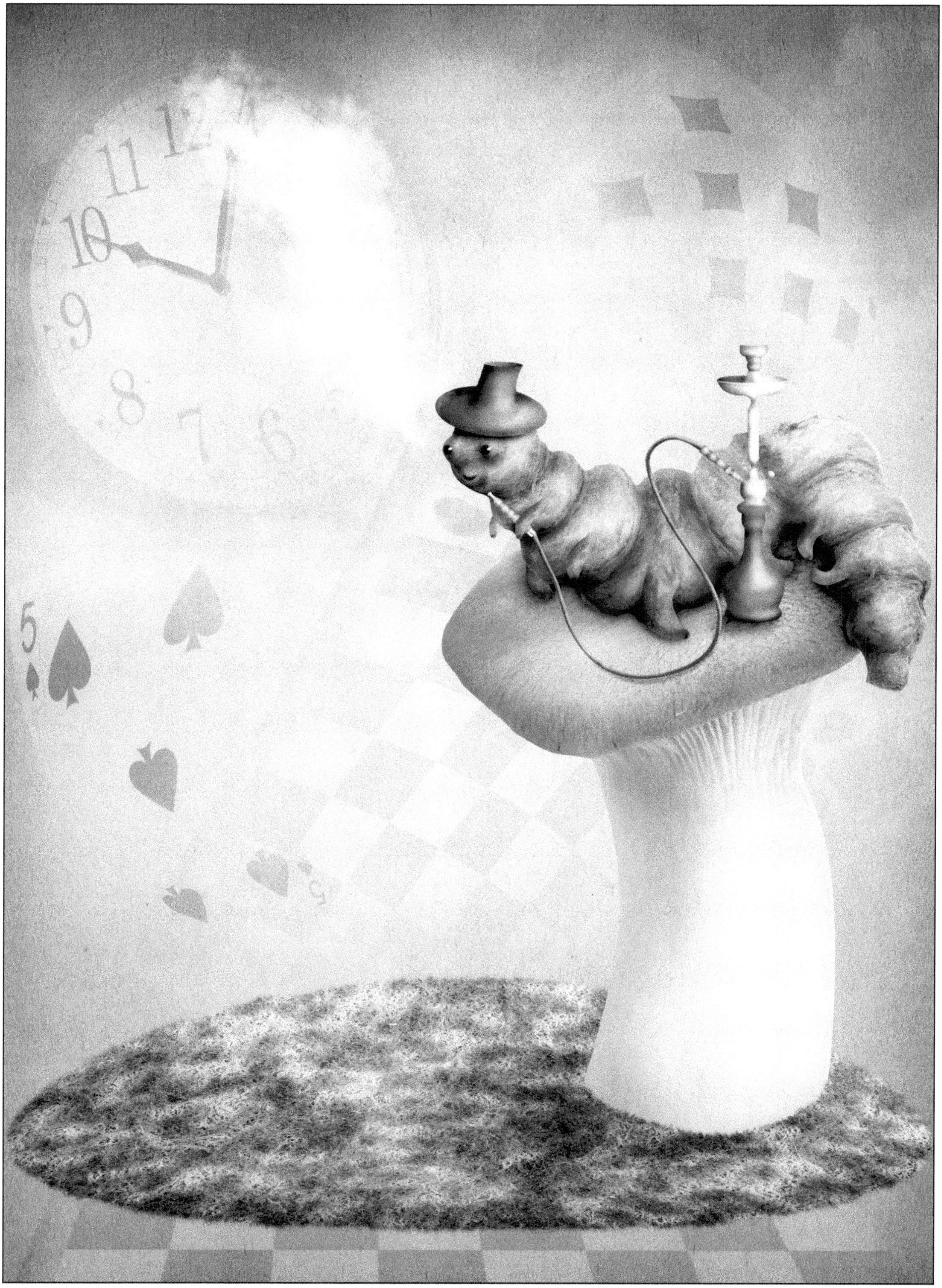

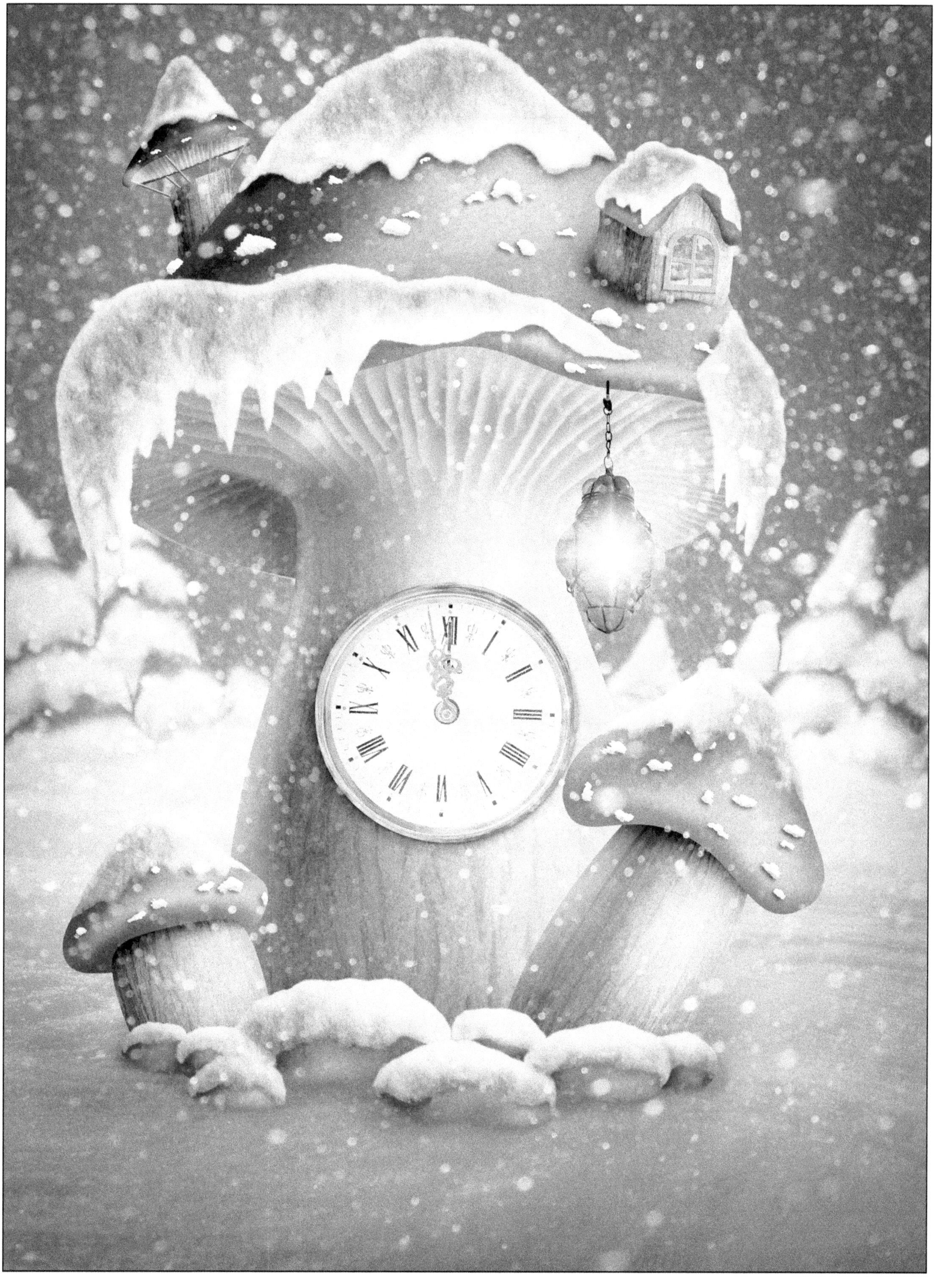

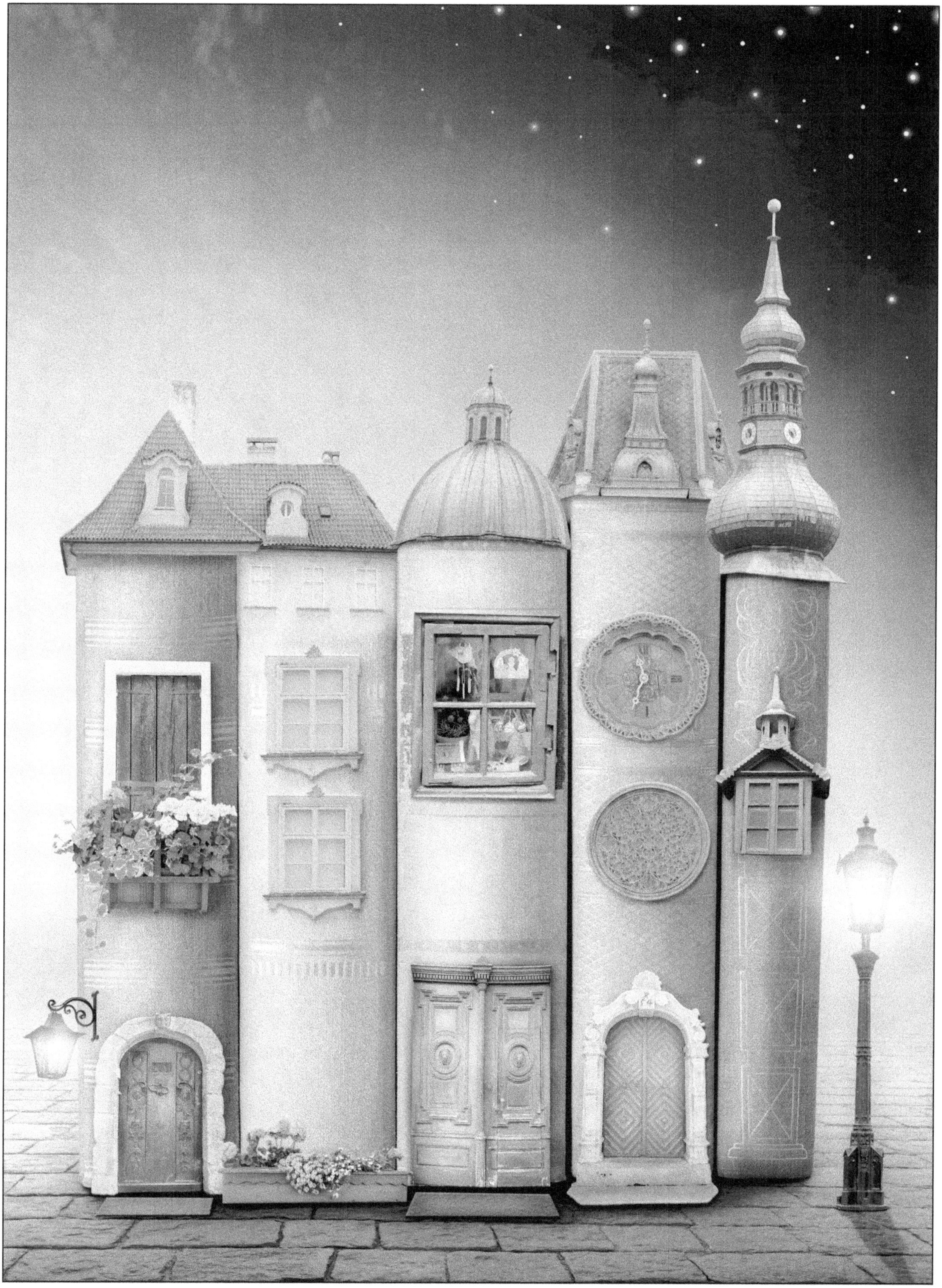

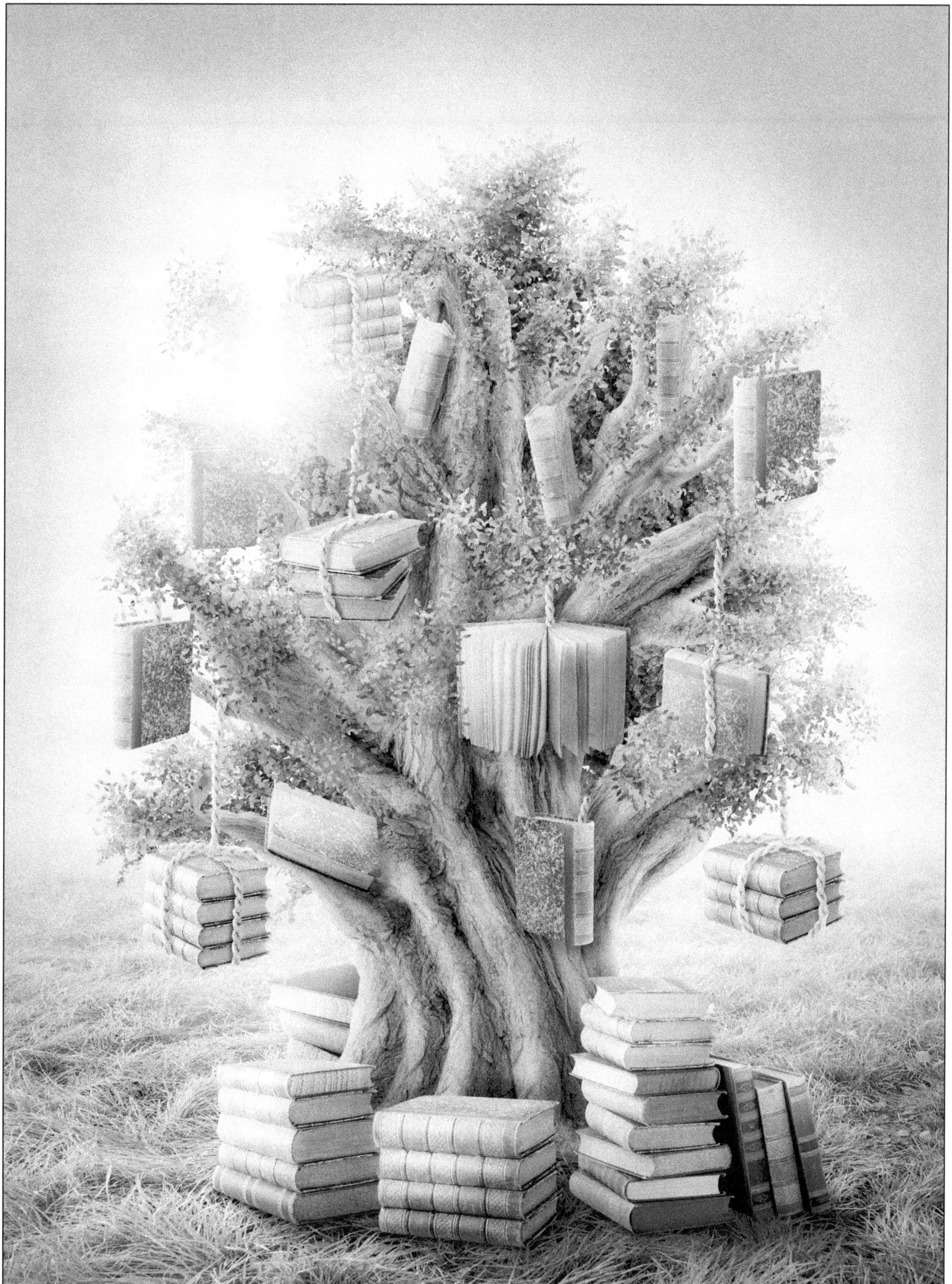

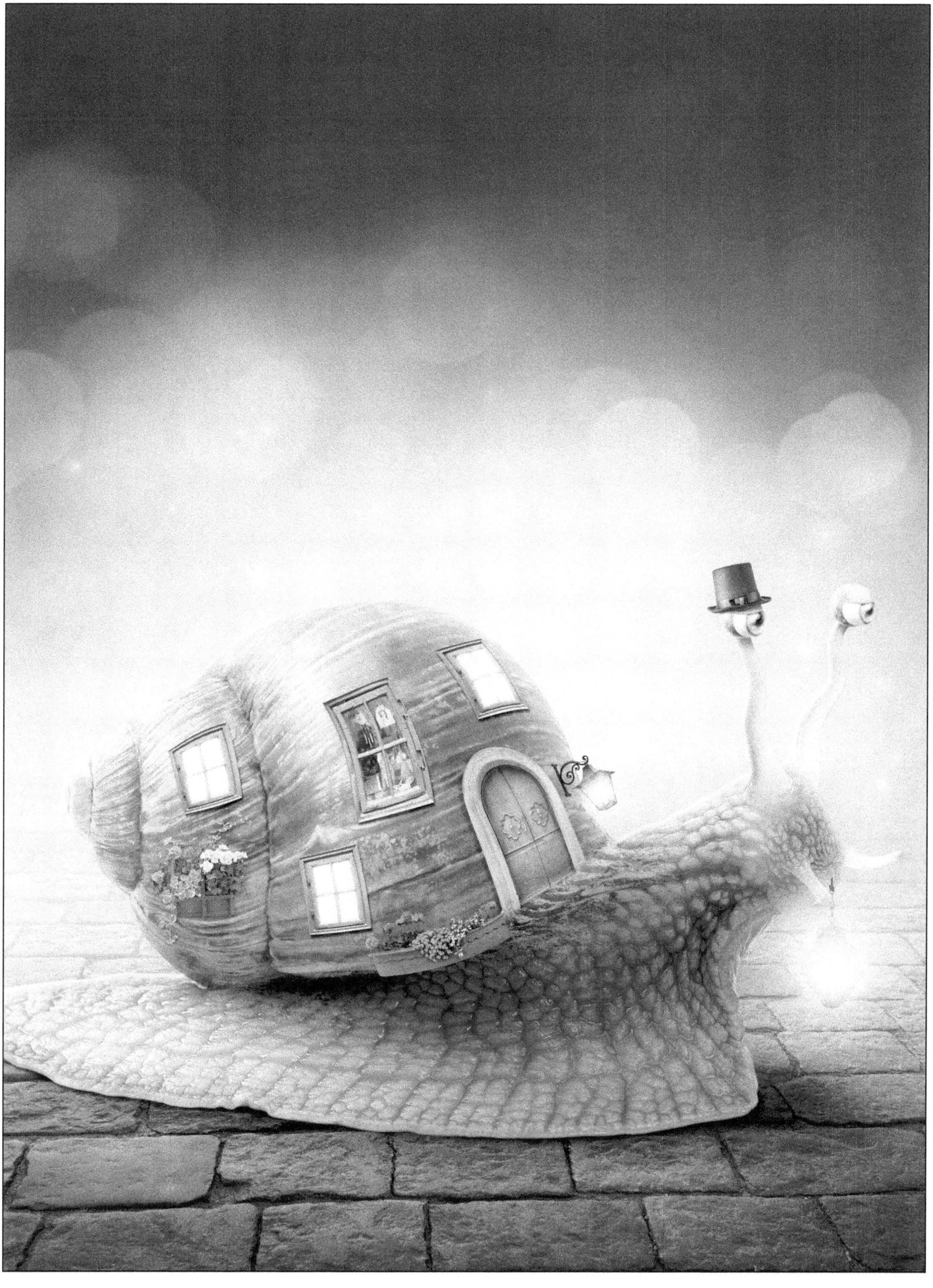

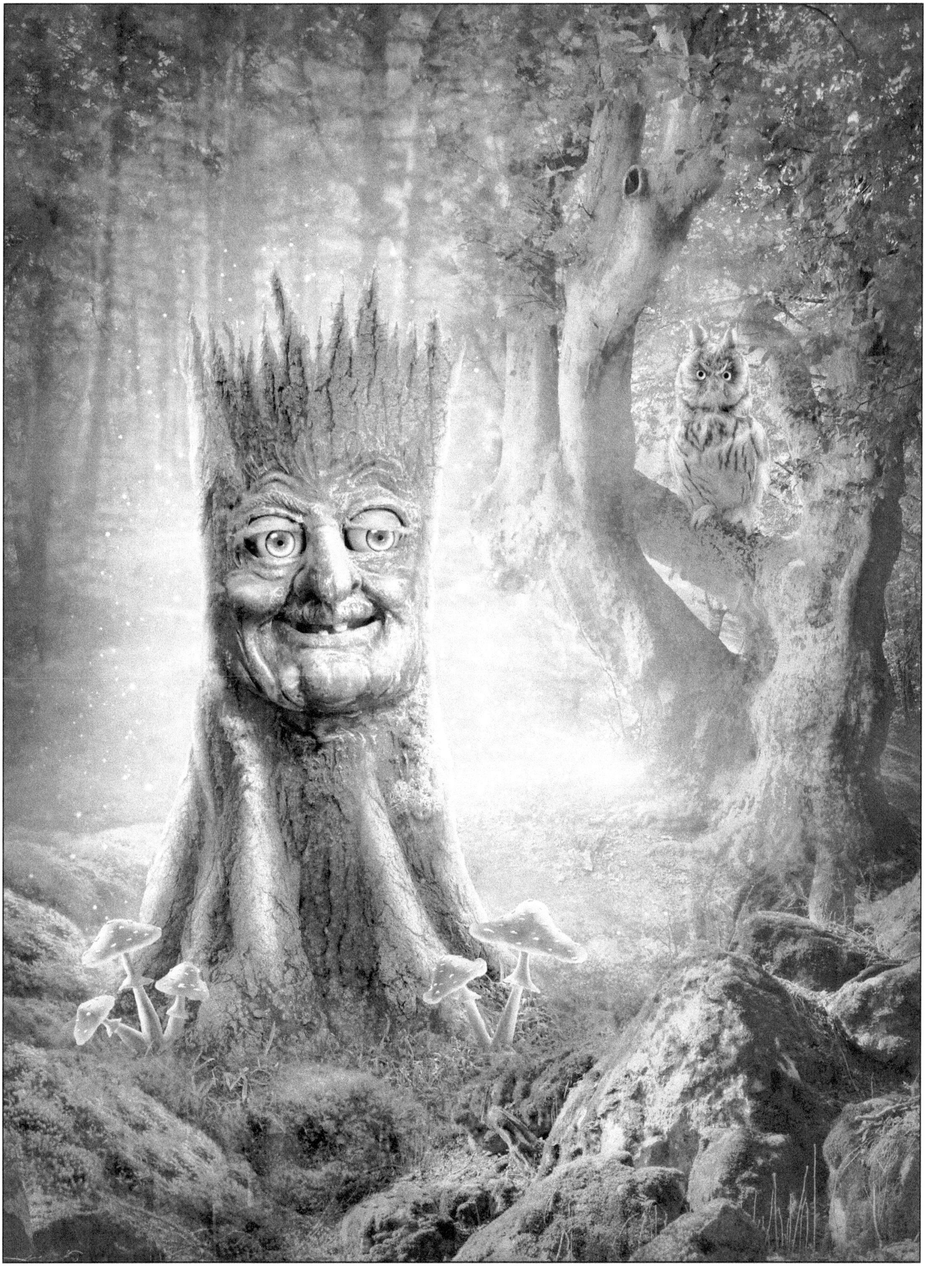

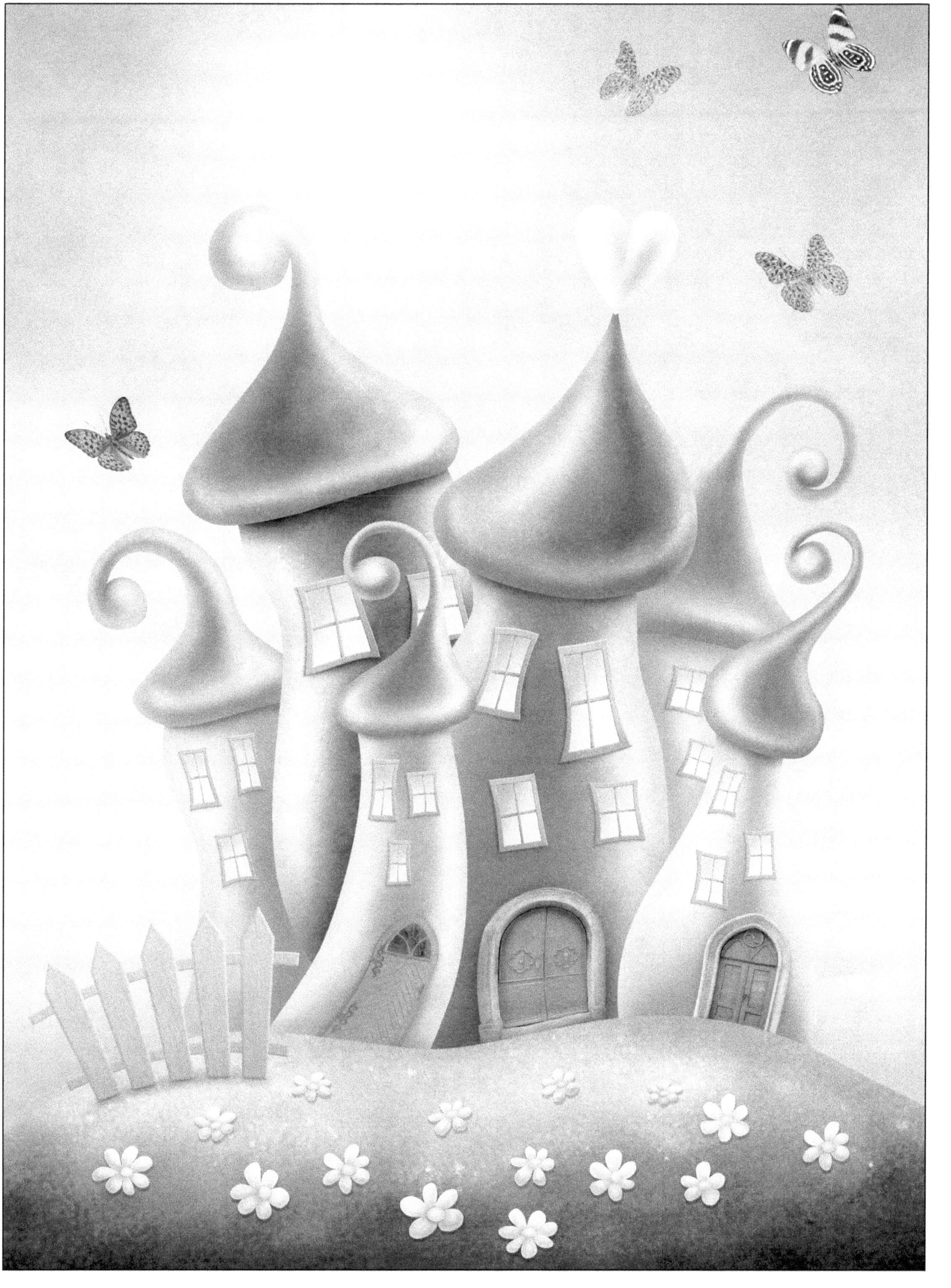

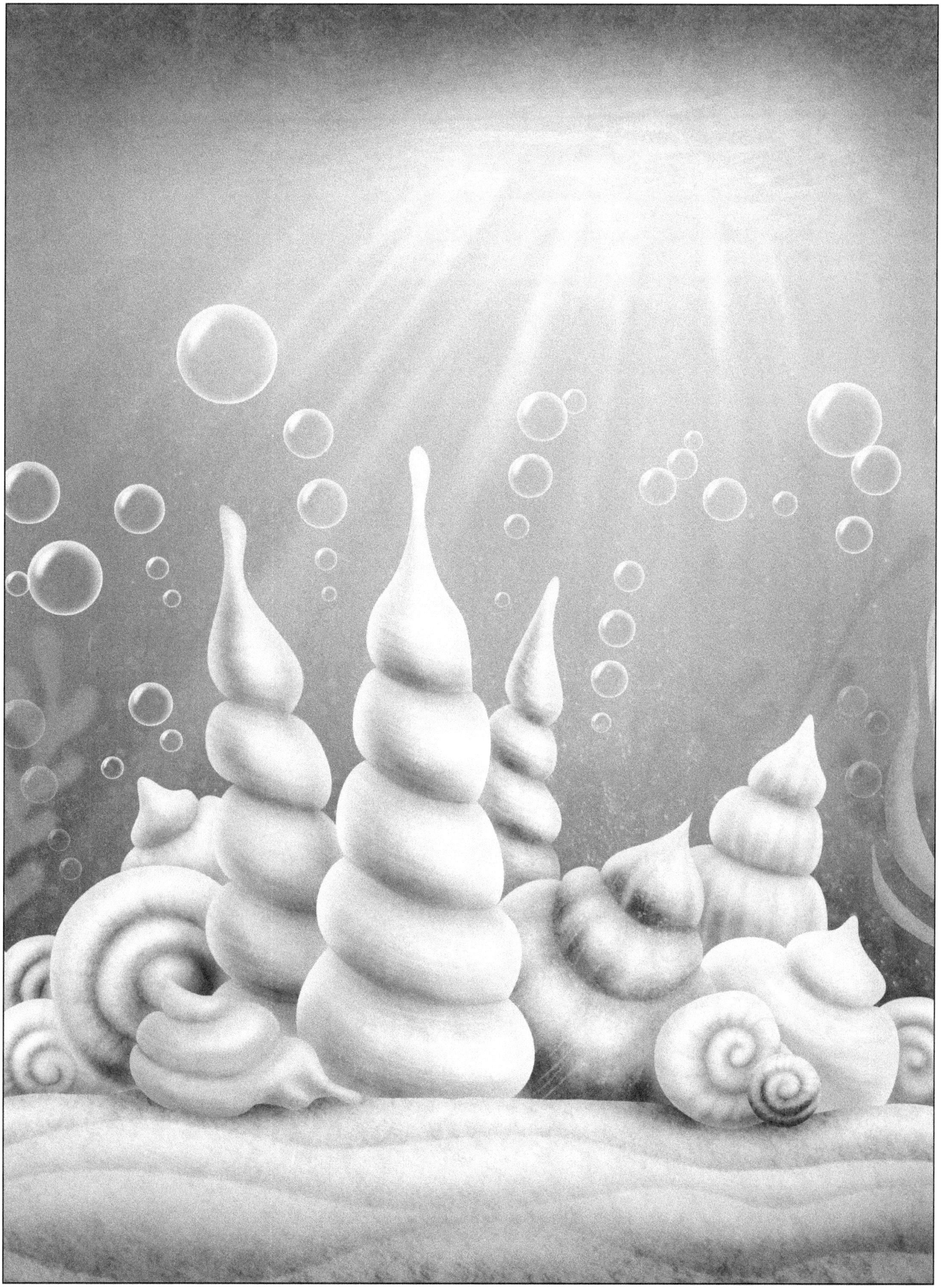

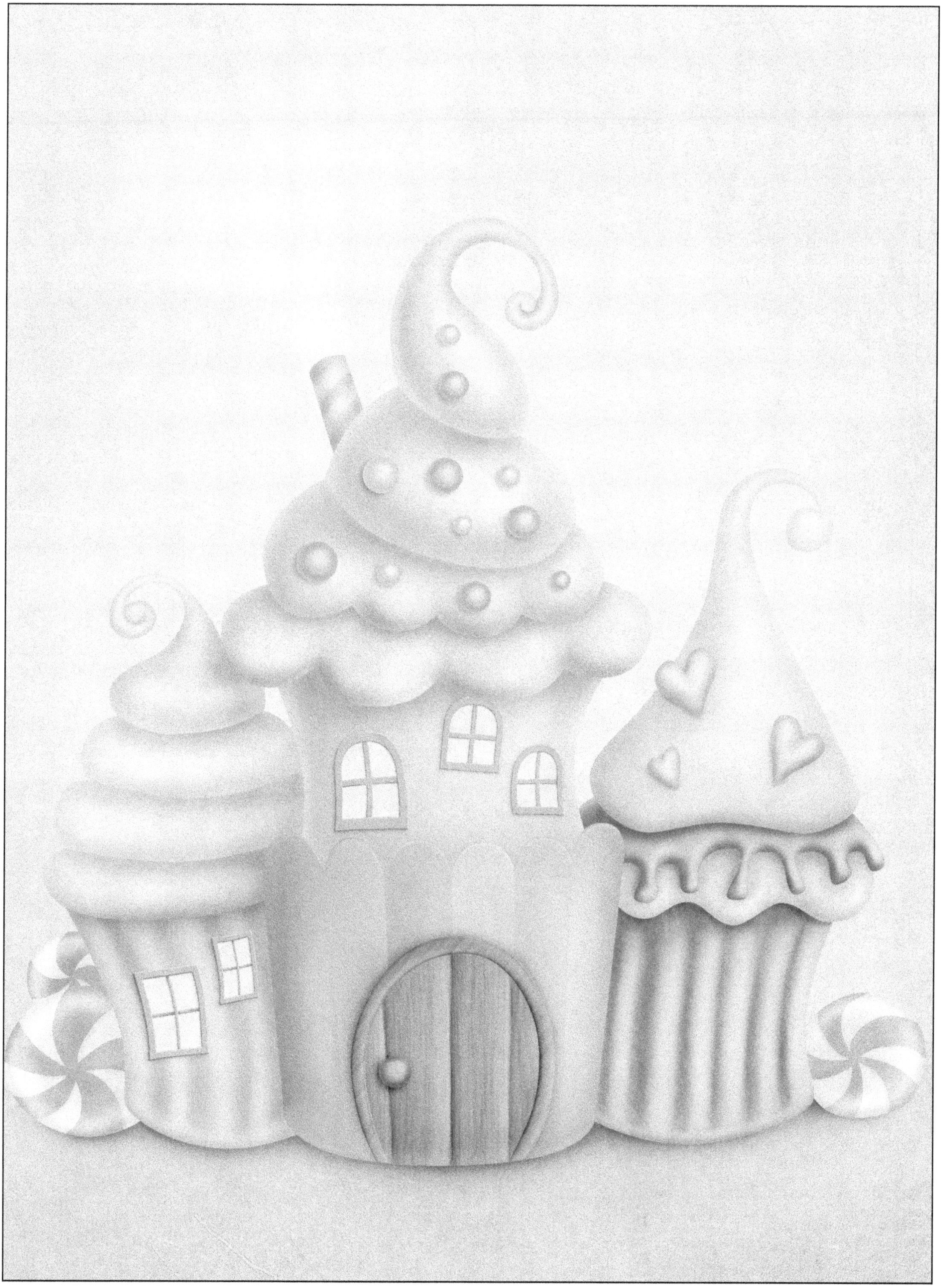

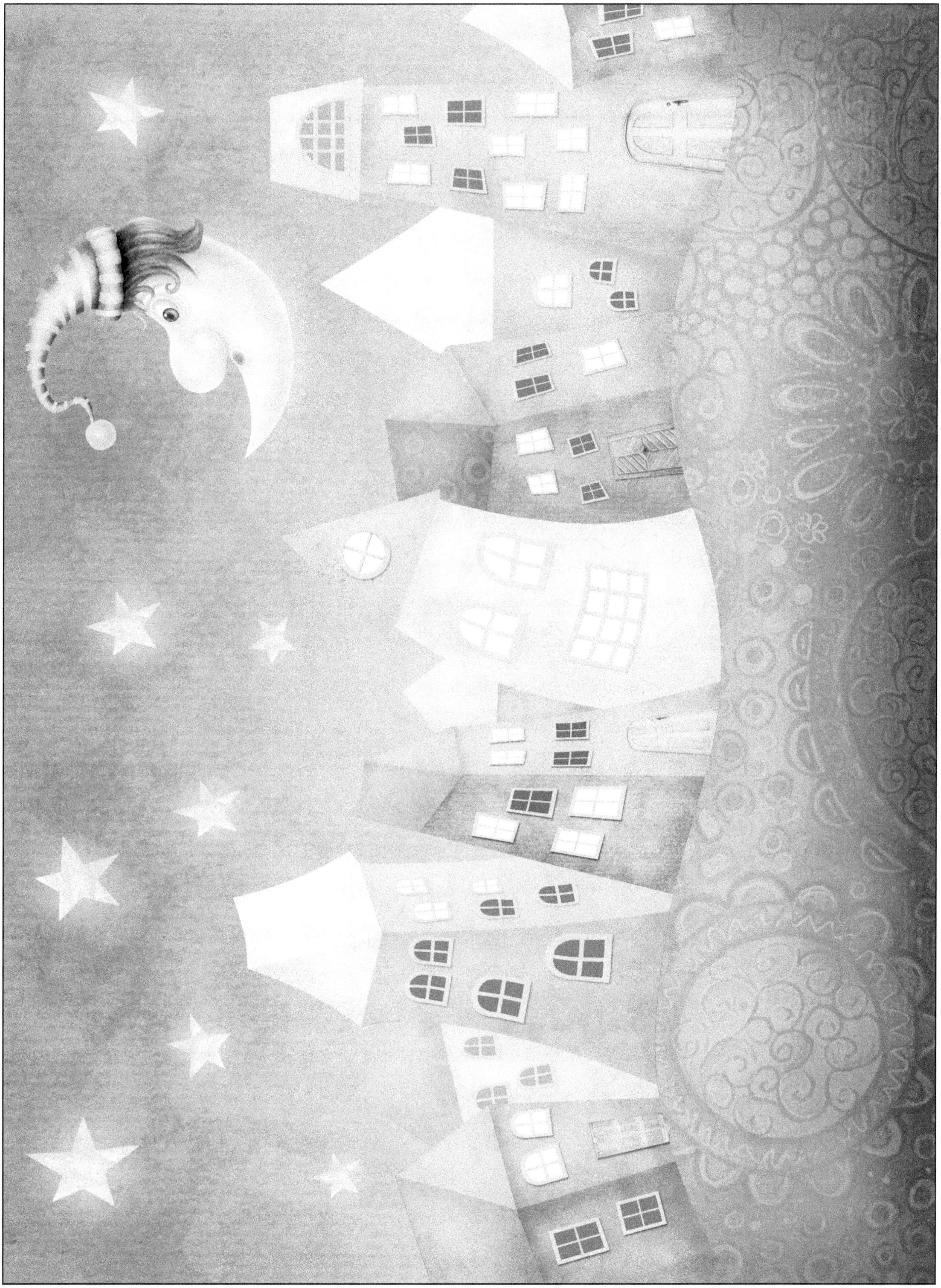

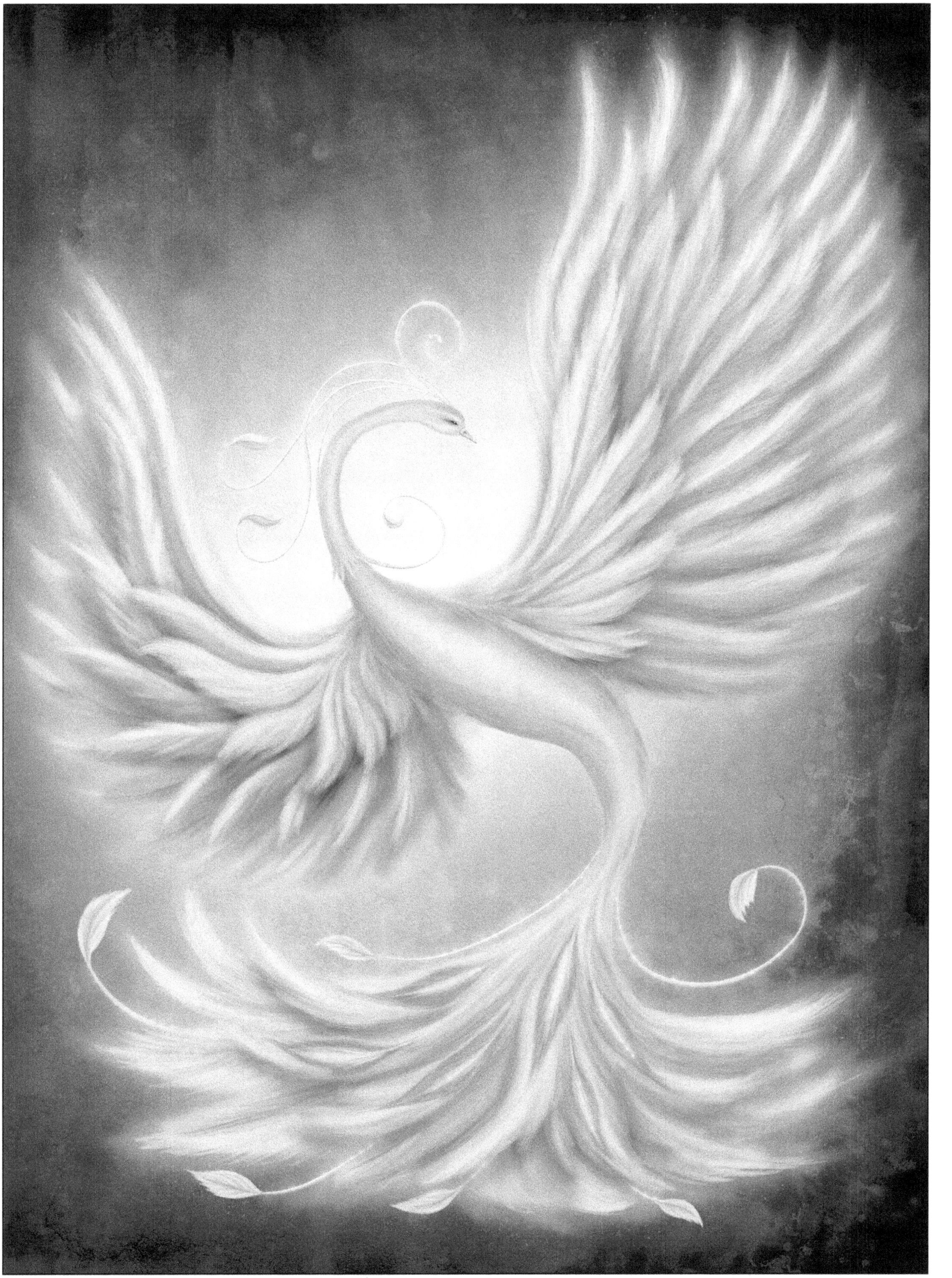

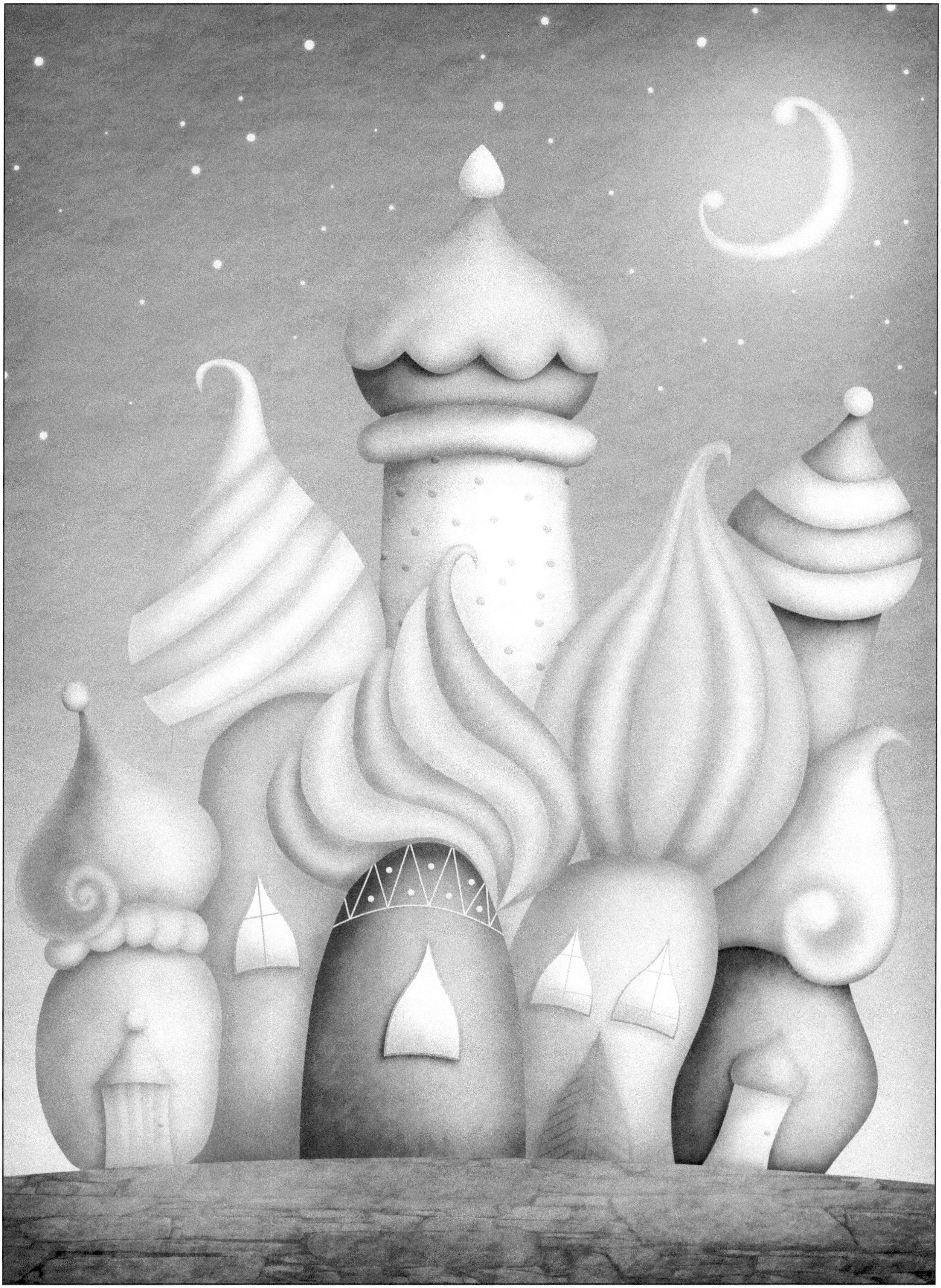

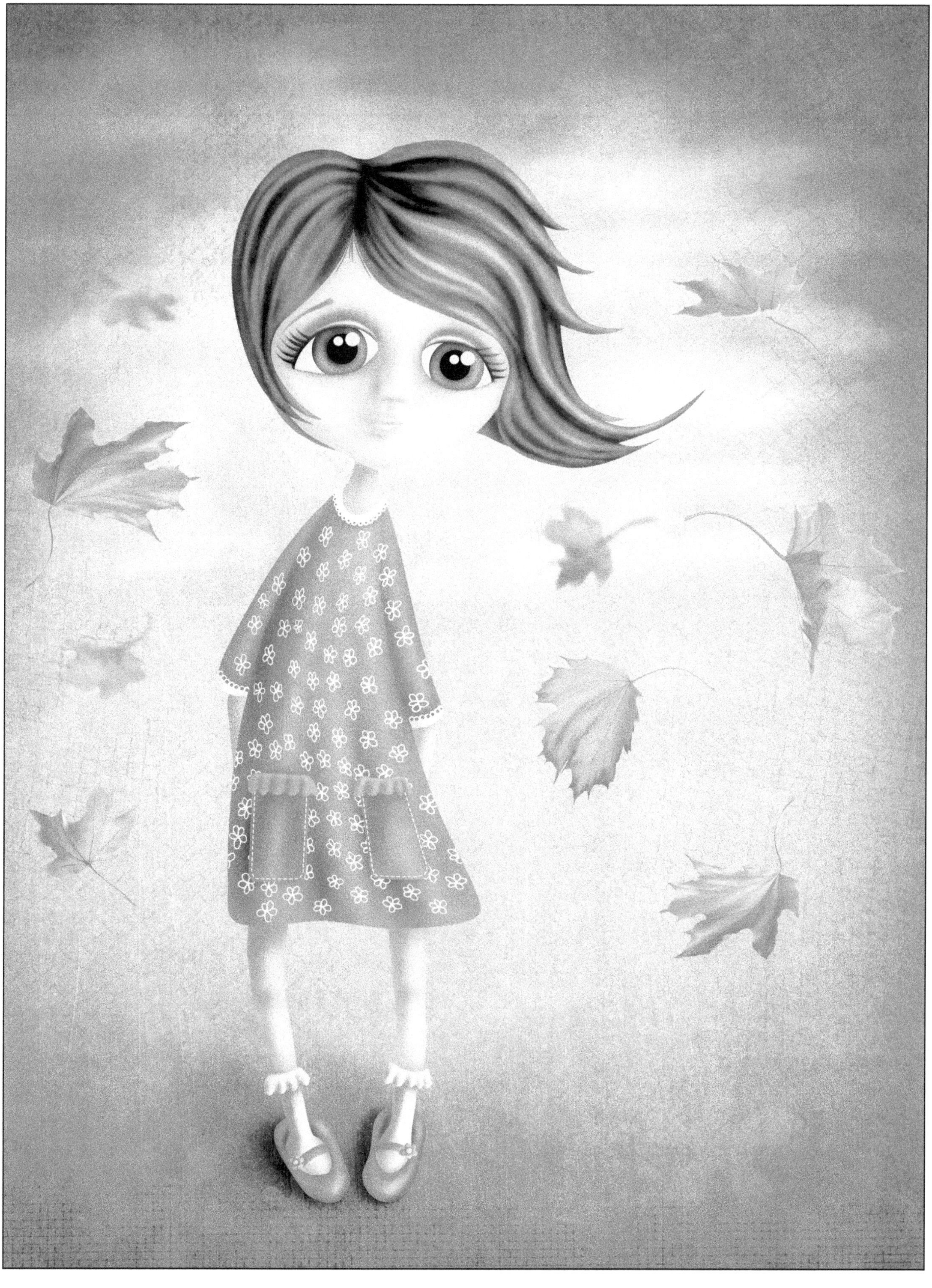

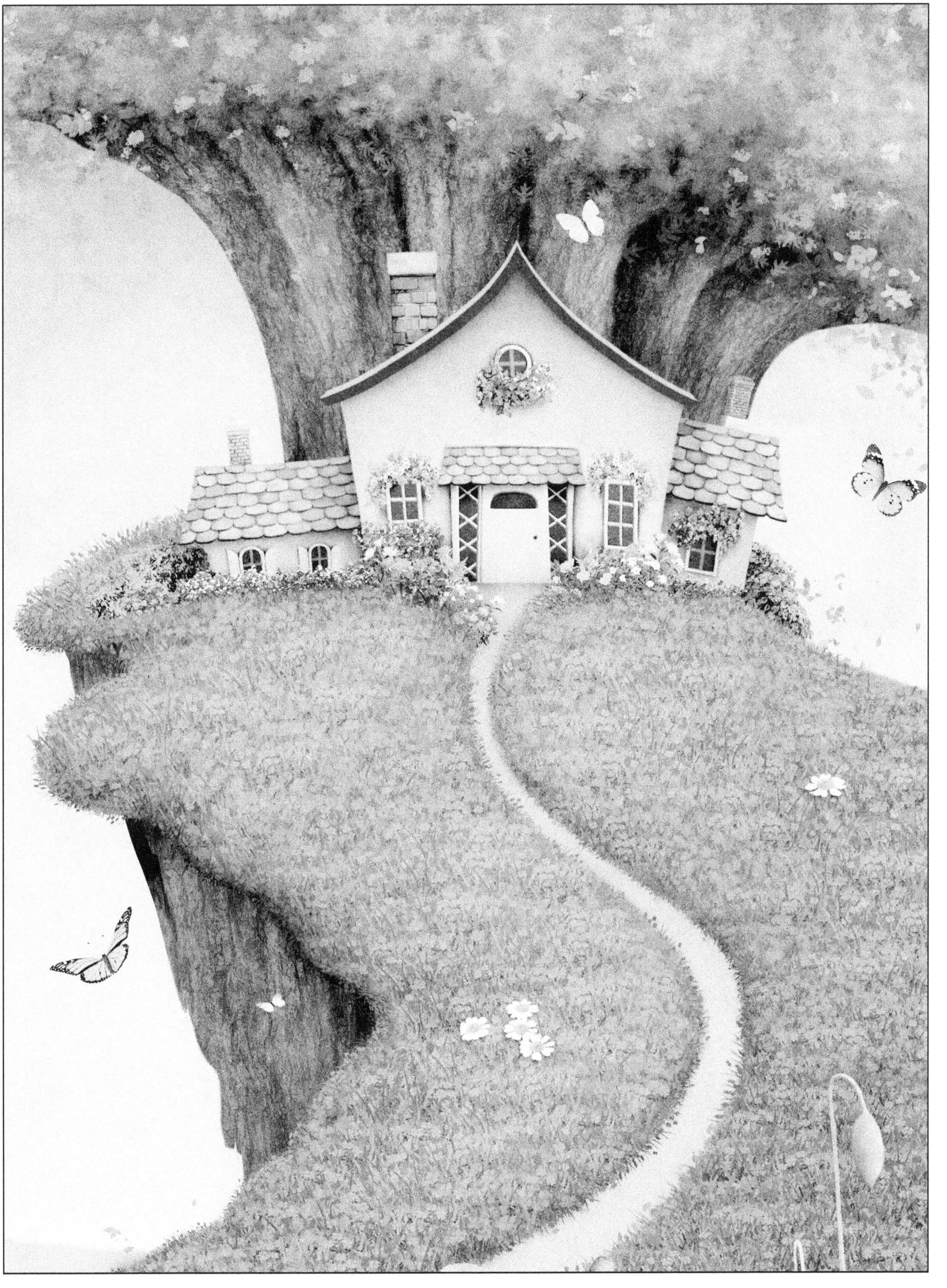

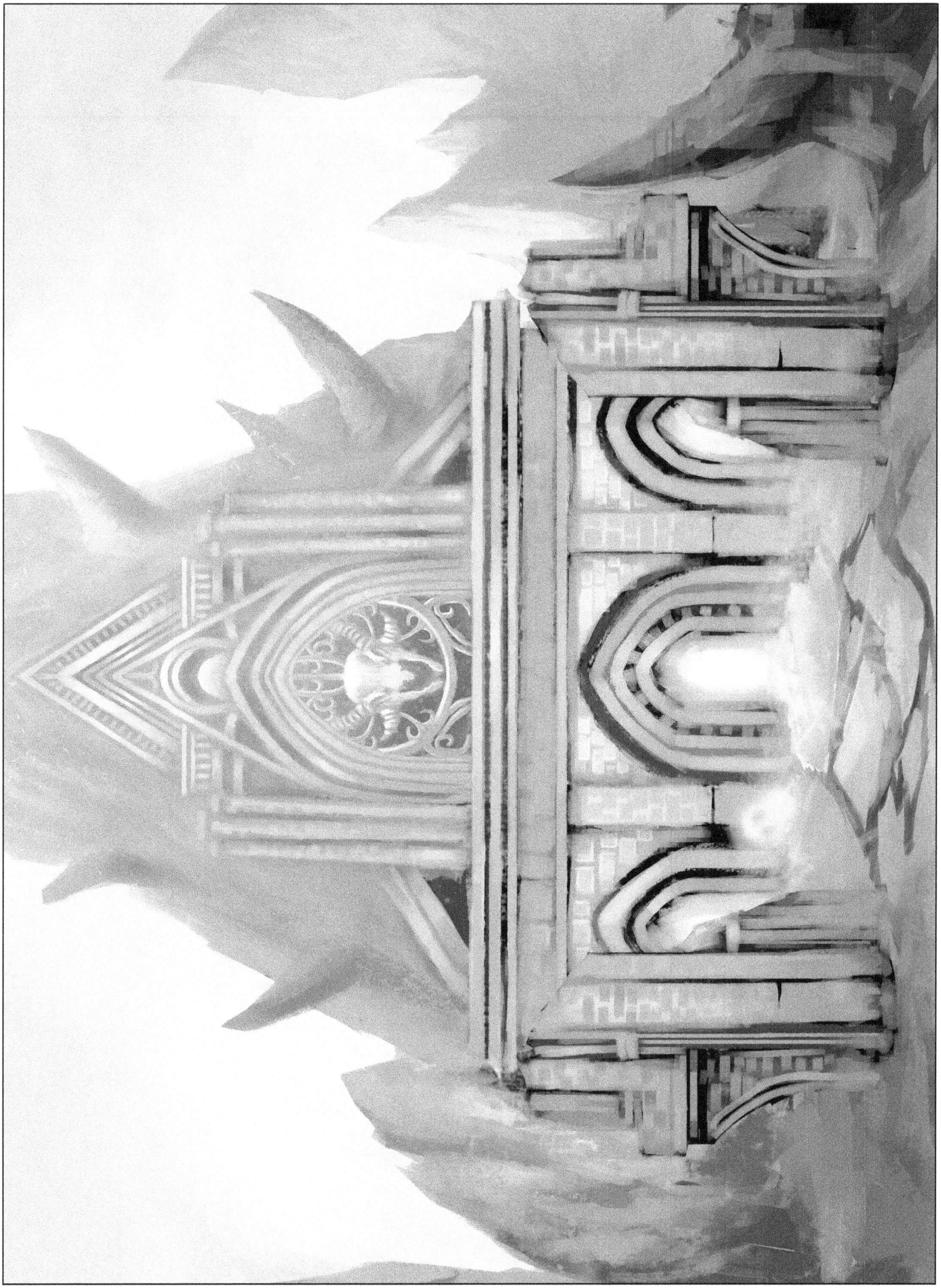

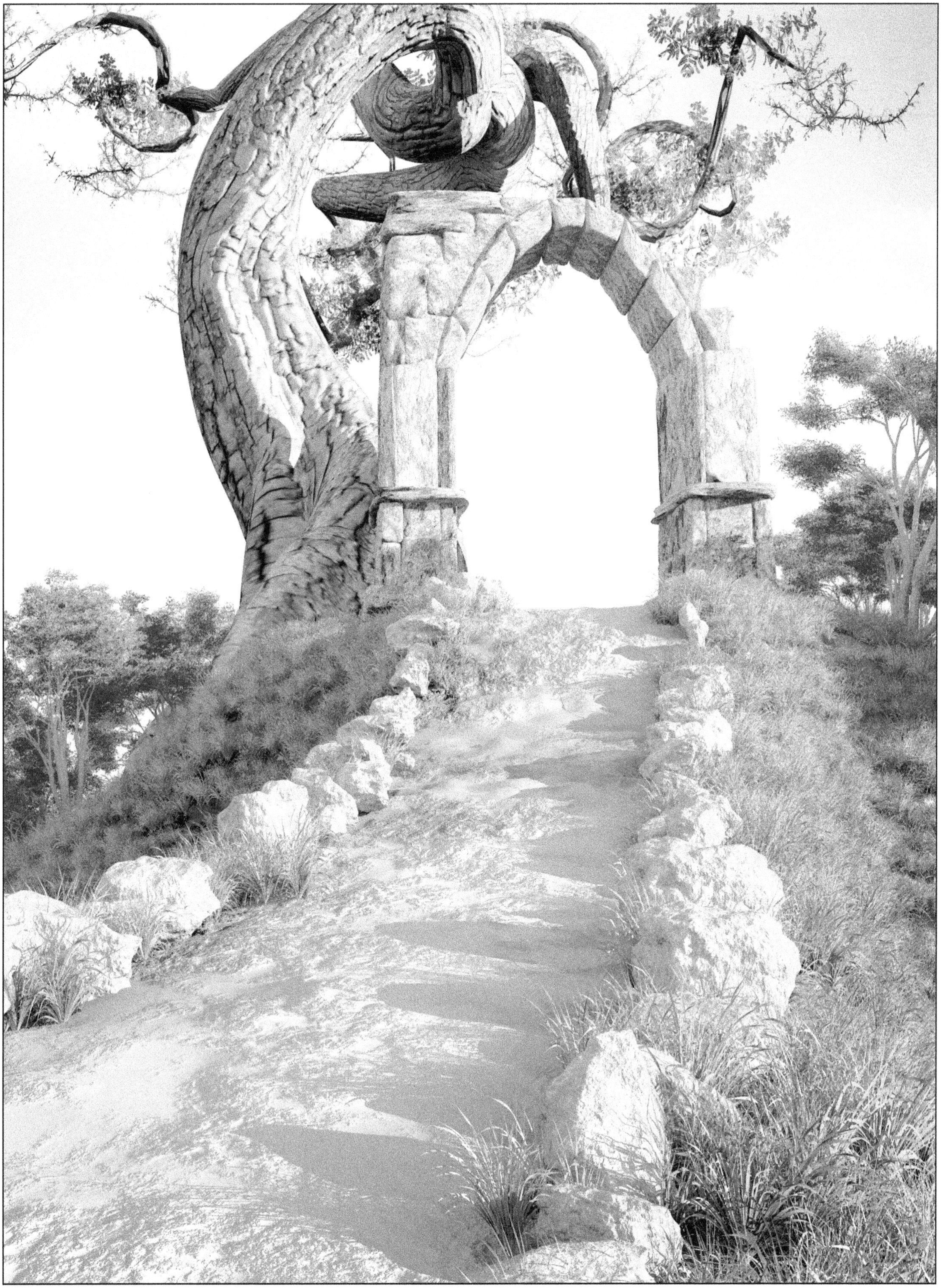

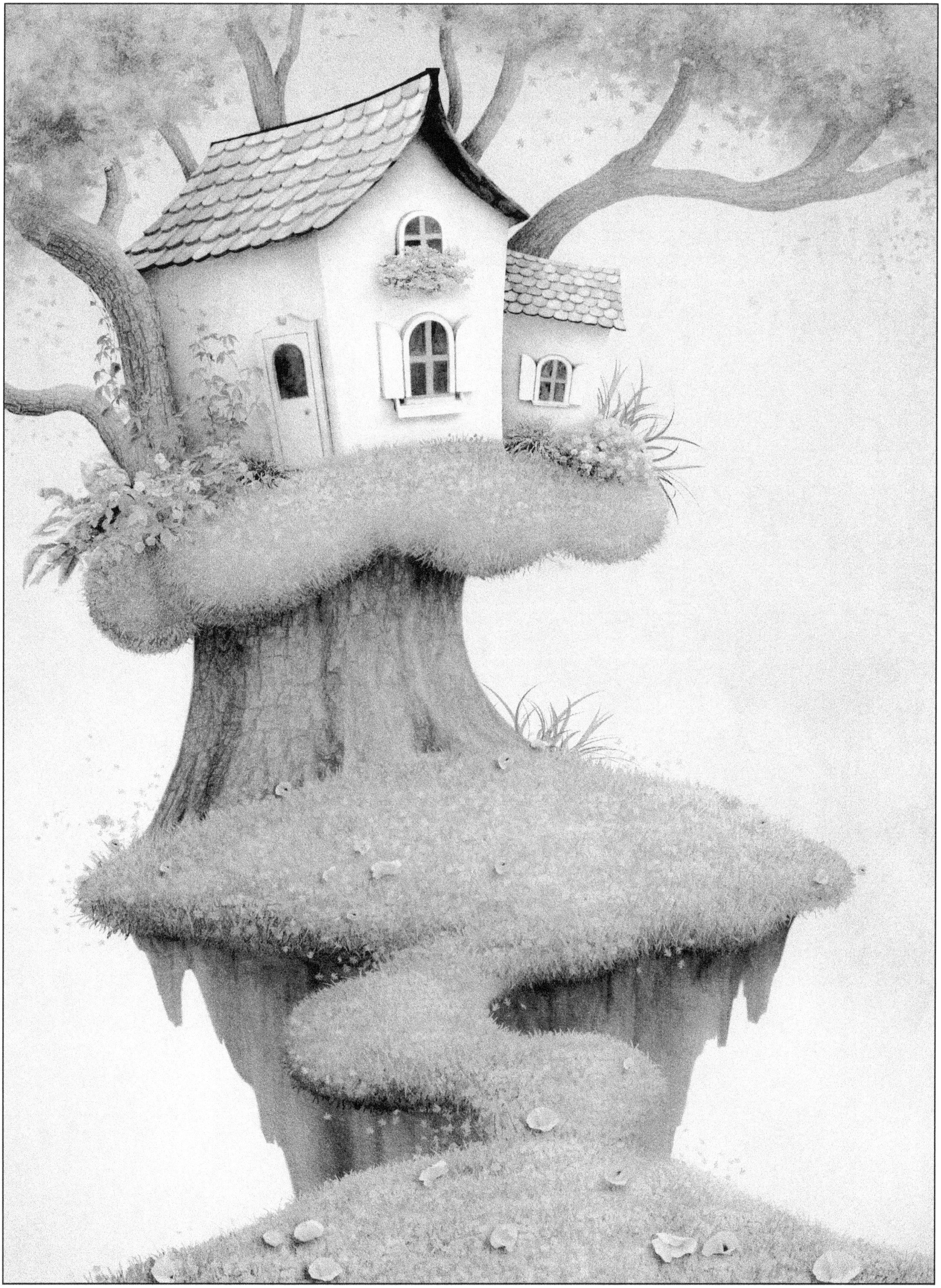

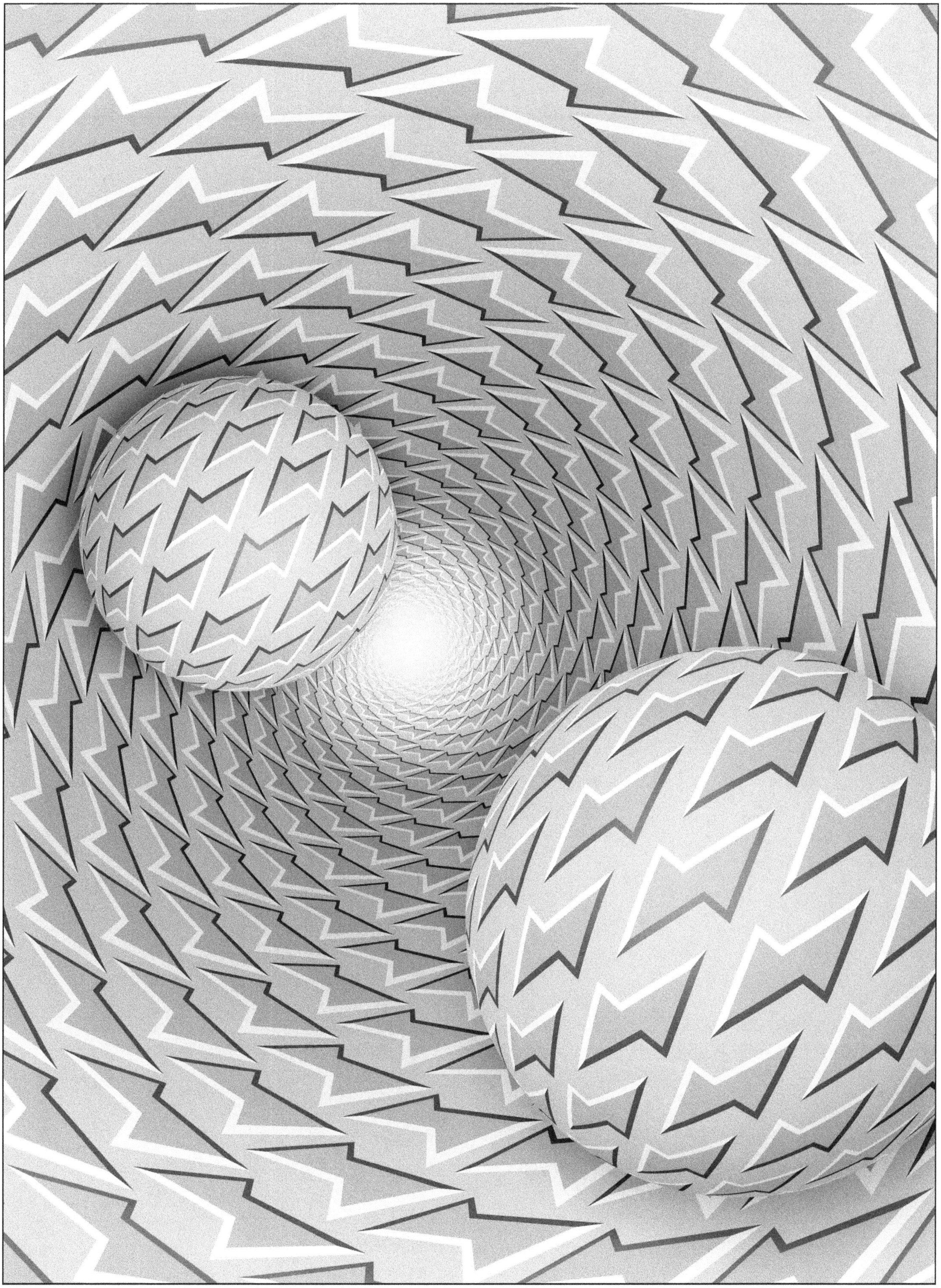

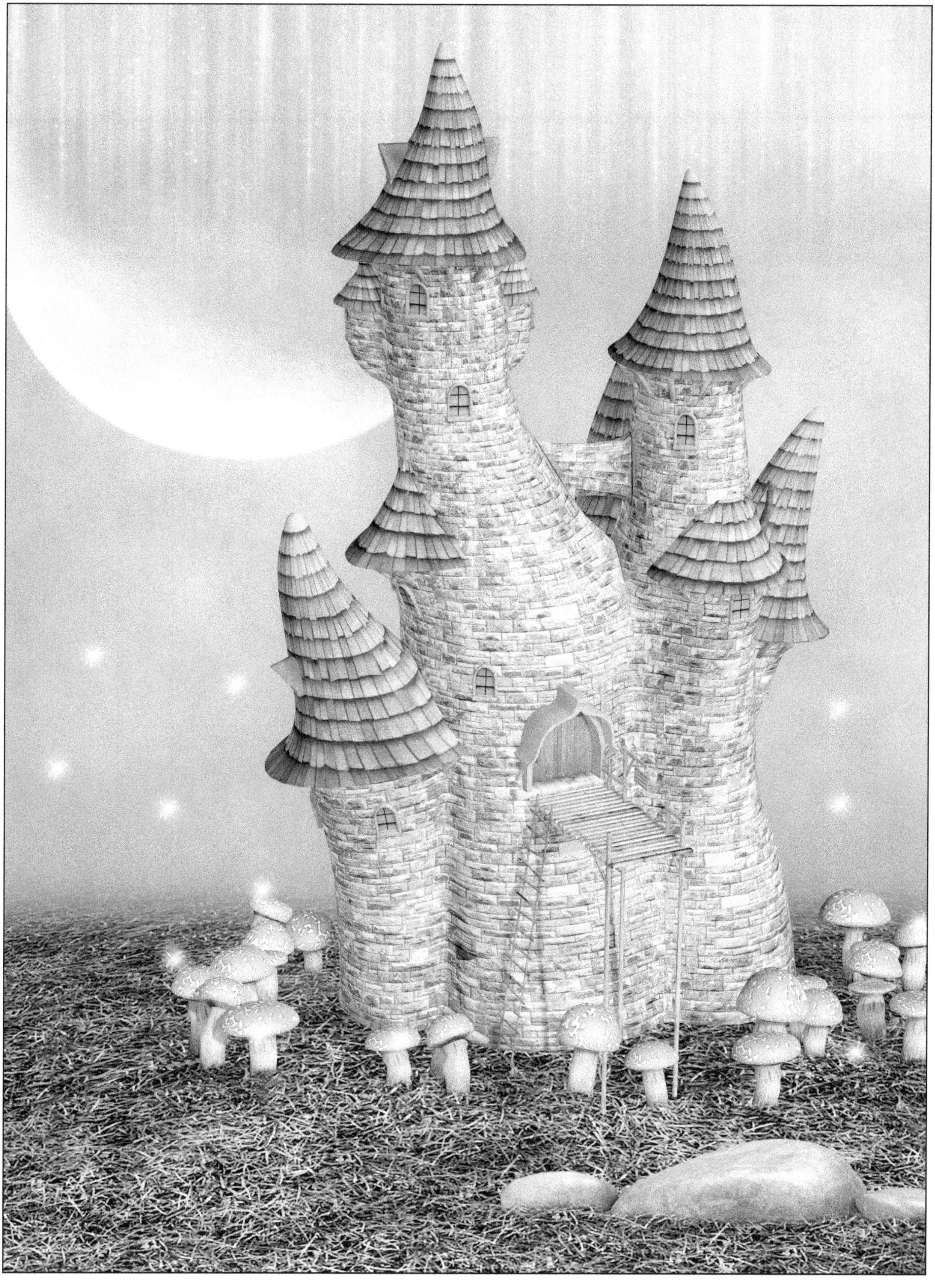

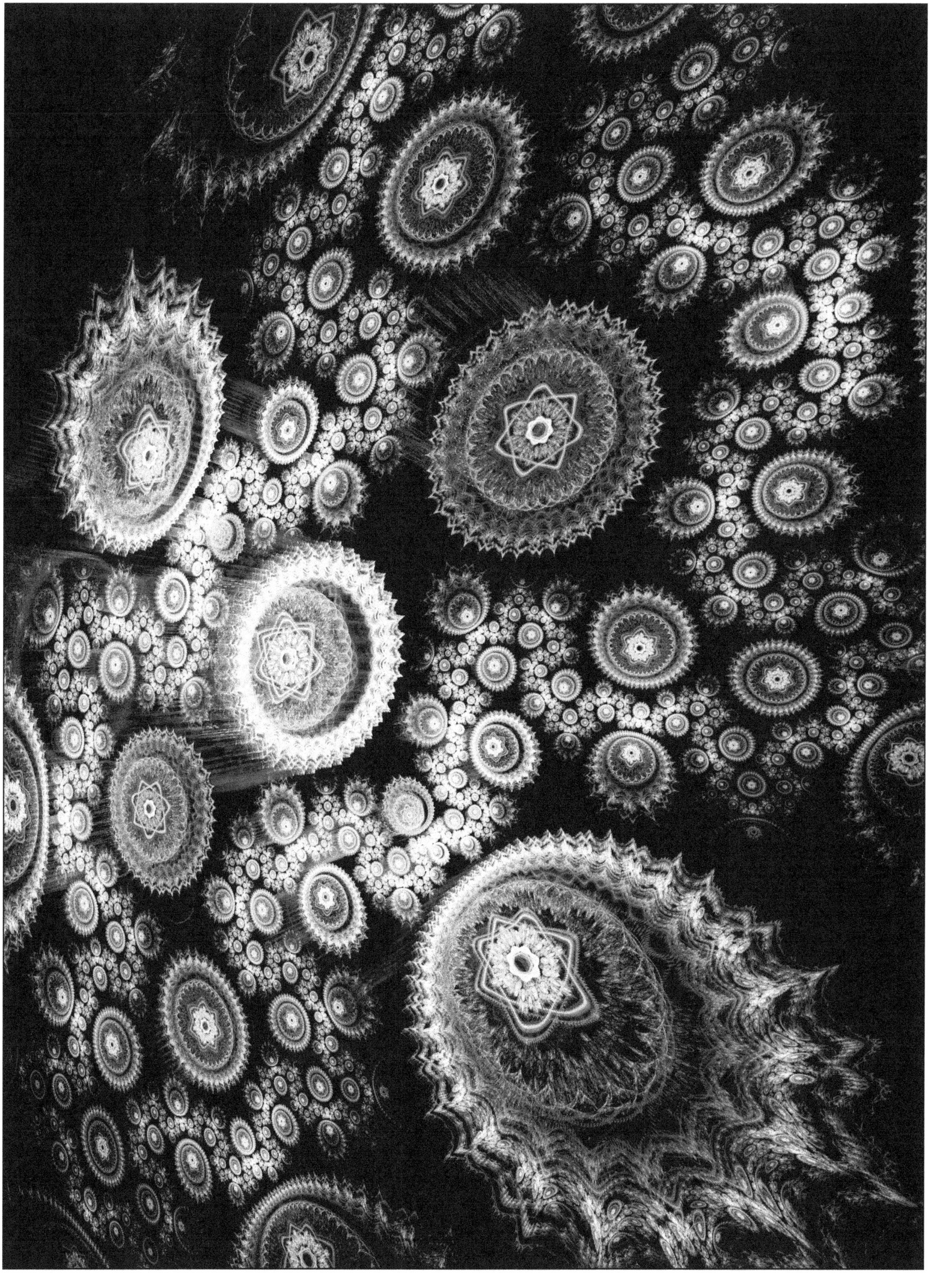

FREE DOWNLOAD

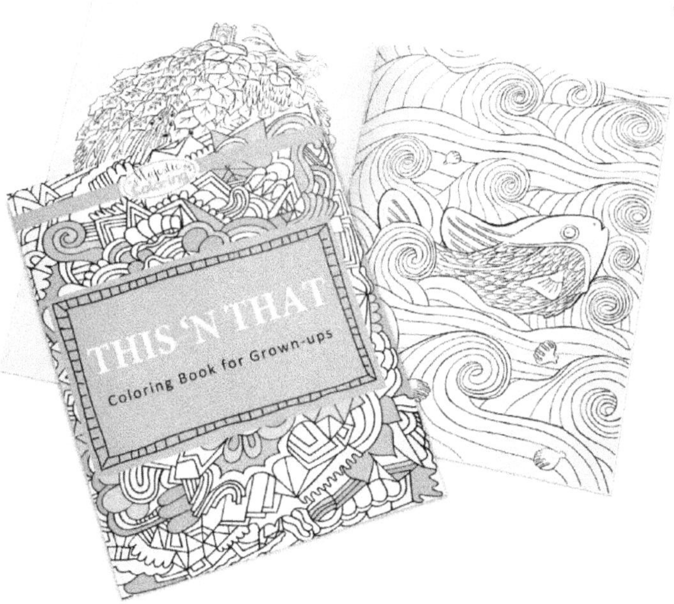

12 FUN DESIGNS FOR YOUR COLORING ENJOYMENT!

This 'n That Coloring Book for Grown-Ups is bundled up in one convenient PDF file to download and print at your leisure.

Sign up for our Majestic Coloring mailing list and get a free copy of **This 'n That Coloring Book for Grown-Ups**.

Click here to get started
http://majesticcoloring.com/thisnthat-free

www.ingramcontent.com/pod-product-compliance
Lightning Source LLC
Chambersburg PA
CBHW080602190526
45169CB00007B/2852
* 9 7 8 1 5 3 3 5 9 1 3 8 8 *